AT
SCHOOL

First published 2010 by Zero to Ten

© Zero to Ten Ltd 2022 this edition

ISBN 9781840897746 hardback
ISBN 9781840897791 paperback

Écoles du monde © 2007 Editions
Milan

English text: Paul Harrison

At school. – (Window on the world)
   1. Schools–Pictorial works–
   Juvenile literature.
   I. Series
   371-dc22

Picture Credits

Sandrine and Alain Moreno: 4, 15

Bios-phone: 10, 12 (Jean-Jacques
Alcalay), 21 (Christophe Courteau)

Corbis: 5 (Remin Benali),
7 (Christian Kober/ Robert Harding
World Imagery), 8, 25 (Gideon
Mendel), 13 (M. Desjeux Bernard),
14 (Ricardo Azoury), 16 (TWPhoto),
18 Michael S. Yamashita),
19 (Lindsay Hebberd), 23 (K.M.
Westermann), 26 (Karen Kasmauski),
27 (Michael Prince), 28 (Will &
Deni Mclntyre), 29 (Anders Ryman),
30 (Stephanie Maze).

Explorer/ Hoaqui/ Jacana:
Cover (Michel Renaudeau), Title
page, 24 (Bettina Brinkmann),
6 (Gerard), 9 (R. Mattes), 11 (Michel
Renaudeau), 17 (Thierry Borredon).

Rapho: 20 (Olivier Föllmi).

Top: 22 (Robert Tixador).

AT SCHOOL

Going to school, but not on the bus ... all of these
Indian children go to school on one bike!

The bell has gone, it's time for school. These Vietnamese children wait patiently in a line.

Do you wear a uniform when you go to school?

Does it look smart like the ones these boys in the **United Kingdom** wear?

These children from Brazil speak two different languages, so lessons are taught in Guaraní and Portuguese.

In Niger too this school is outside and the teacher uses a rock as a chalkboard.

If the weather is dry why not sit outside? These children in India are wrapped up nice and warm while they learn.

Imagine if your desk and chair were made out of mud! In this school in Mali that's exactly what happens.

There are no chairs or desks, but this is still a school. In this part of Rajasthan they all sit on the floor.

These children in Senegal learn to write on slates. When they get the answers right they wipe the slate clean.

Do you know the answer? Then put your hand in the air!
These Chinese children all want to have a go.

Time for lessons so put away your things. The Japanese girls hang their hats in a line.

Point to the letters as you say the alphabet. This **Ethiopian** boy is showing what he knows.

It's lunchtime in Japan, so the books are tidied away. No need to move though – the children eat at their desks.

Little people need little tables and chairs to sit at; this German canteen is perfect for young children.

In China lunch is over and it's time for a sleep. See the young children tucked up cosy and warm.

Reach way up high, then squat down low –
these Indian children are doing their exercises.

Big pictures on a wall are easy to see, even for the children
at the back of this Ethiopian class.

Now for the children's turn – this Nigerian girl writes about a giraffe.

It's time for art so let's go outside.

These Japanese children draw what they see.

We're on a school trip to visit a palace.

These Thai children take lots of notes.

Break time! The French children rush outside to play
on bikes and hoops.

Or would you like to play football with these Kenyan children? Disabled or not, everybody joins in the fun.

These Japanese children sing along with the teacher, but one little boy thinks the songs are too loud!

Headphones and microphones, what's going on here?
These Chinese children learn a new language.

The bell rings – school's over! These American children all rush to go home.

It's a long way home for this Bolivian boy, so he walks with his mother past the wide, winding river.

Just because you're at home, it doesn't mean you stop learning. This Japanese boy does homework with his grandma.

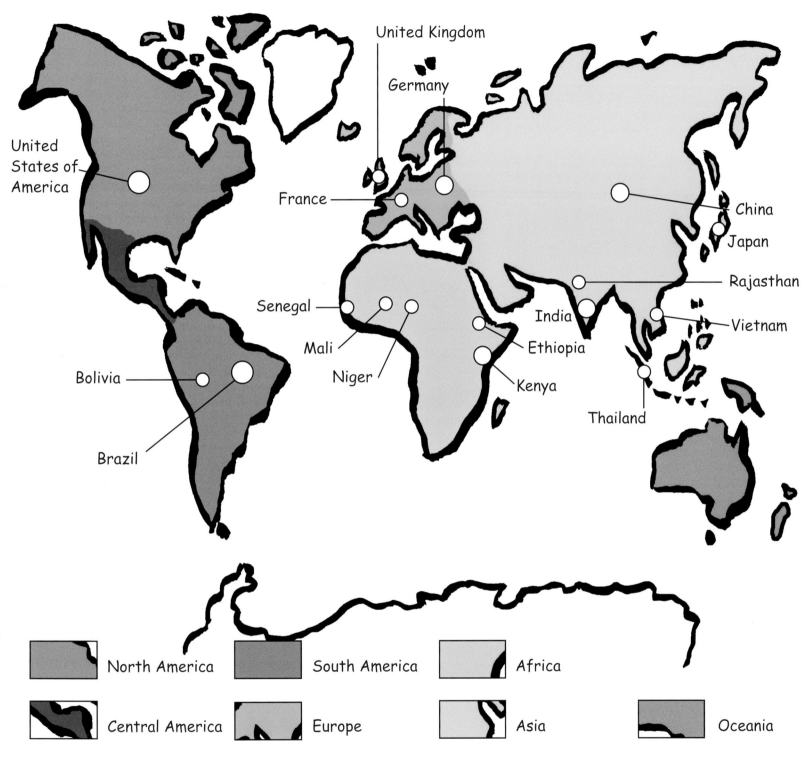

United Kingdom

Germany

United States of America

France

China

Japan

Rajasthan

Senegal

India

Vietnam

Mali

Ethiopia

Bolivia

Niger

Kenya

Brazil

Thailand

North America

South America

Africa

Central America

Europe

Asia

Oceania

If you want to know where in the world the pictures are taken you can use this map. Look out for the words in colour – they are an important clue!

Other titles in the series:

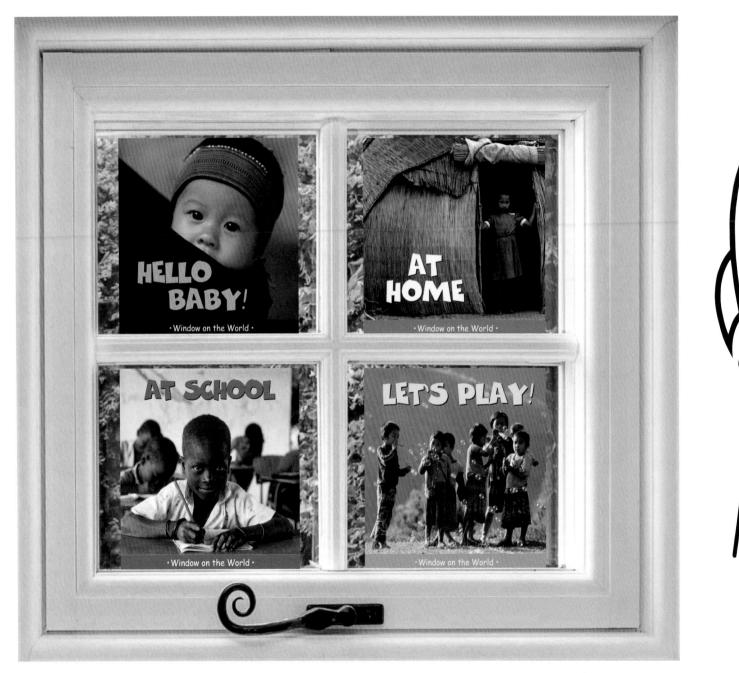

HELLO BABY!
· Window on the World ·

AT HOME
· Window on the World ·

AT SCHOOL
· Window on the World ·

LET'S PLAY!
· Window on the World ·